Situation

A Guide to the Appointment Process in
the Church of England

David Parrott

Barking Area CME Adviser, Diocese of Chelmsford

David Field

Formerly Patronage Secretary of the Church Pastoral Aid Society

Associate Ministi = 2nd curacy)
Made up - ① reed b ministi oH than being th incumben'.
ie expeunce but not in charge.

Team Rectu + Team Vicca
7yu.

GROVE BOOKS LIMITED
RIDLEY HALL RD CAMBRIDGE CB3 9HU

Contents

The Cover Illustration is by Peter Ashton

First Impression March 1996
Reprinted with corrections April 1999
Revised Edition April 2005
ISSN 0144-171X
ISBN 1 85174 311 1

Introduction

1

> ## Help!
> - The vicar is leaving and you are a member of the PCC during the vacancy.
> - You are ordained, looking for a new post and wondering how the system works.
> - You are a patron and the benefice where you have a right of presentation has become vacant.
> - You have some diocesan responsibility in the appointment process and are not completely sure how your role relates to others.

This booklet is for you. It is an attempt to review the process of making appointments to incumbent posts in the Church of England and to explain how the system works and where various responsibilities lie. It is not intended to be a definitive interpretation of the law in this area. Such things come in tomes, not booklets. Its aim is simply to describe how the legal procedures work out in practice from the different standpoints of those most involved in the process.

This is a tall order, because the system itself is by no means clear or uniform. The legislation that covers most appointments is the Patronage (Benefices) Measure 1986. Even this Measure, however, does not apply in every case.[1]

It is worth adding that this booklet deals only with the process of appointing *vicars*, *rectors* and *priests-in-charge* in the Church of England. Curates and team vicars are selected in different ways, as are ministers in churches of other denominations.

No-one would dream of inventing the process we describe if it did not exist already. Some find its complexities both anachronistic and frustrating. Nonetheless, once understood, it has considerable latent merits. Hopefully this booklet will encourage those who find themselves involved to understand the way the system operates a little better, to trust those who have interacting roles more fully, and—above all—to listen for God's voice with greater discernment. The church, after all, is his; and the bottom line which we all acknowledge is that he is not bound by any system which Synod or Parliament may impose.

2

The Appointment Process and Key Players

A Tripod of Responsibility

Whenever a new vicar or rector is to be appointed under the Patronage (Benefices) Measure, three parties are involved. Their roles interact but remain distinct.

- The patron *nominates* a candidate.
- The PCC, through its elected representatives, *affirms* or *vetoes* the patron's nomination. *light t appror!*
- The bishop *institutes.*

The checks and balances this arrangement provides are important. The patron cannot 'put a new vicar in' by himself or herself. The bishop (unless he is also the patron) cannot nominate. And without an appeal to the archbishop—which may fail anyway—neither bishop nor patron can overrule the veto of just one of the PCC's representatives.

These three parties are the key players. Rather like the three legs of a tripod, they can bring stability to the process as a whole.

The Patron

Who are patrons and why are they there? The answer takes us back to Anglo-Saxon times, when individual landowners built churches for those who lived on their estates and provided for clergymen to minister to them. Since then, the roles of the bishop and the PCC have gradually increased in significance, but patrons still retain their rights and responsibilities to nominate a succession of vicars or rectors as vacancies arise.

Until comparatively recently, 'private' patrons were allowed to sell their rights (advowsons). Now they can only give them away. Among the principal beneficiaries are bishops, monasteries, Oxbridge colleges and—since the end of the eighteenth century—patronage trusts.

Evangelicals have been particularly prominent in setting up trusts to take on patronage responsibilities from private individuals. Historically, of course, their primary objective was to ensure the continuance of evangelical teaching at a time when the ecclesiastical establishment was generally hostile to it. Today evangelical trusts account for more than 10% of all patronage. The Church Pastoral Aid Society, which administers three fairly large trusts, has a portfolio second only to the Crown in its size.

Often patronage is shared. Sharing usually results from the uniting of benefices, so it is not unusual to find half a dozen patrons involved when a rural incumbency is vacant. They may operate in turns (which is always the practice when the Crown is included) or jointly. Team rectors are normally appointed by patronage boards chaired by diocesan or area bishops.

The shape which patronage takes depends a great deal, therefore, on the way benefices have come into being and been changed over the years. The main variants are set out in Appendix 1. The patron's power remains considerable. Though both the bishop and the local church's PCC have rights of veto (see below), only the patron has the proactive authority to nominate.

Though both the bishop and the local church's PCC have rights of veto, only the patron has the proactive authority to nominate

One might think that such weighty influence would carry with it continuing obligations, but patrons are no longer financially responsible for the upkeep of 'their' churches or for paying the salaries of 'their' clergy. Nor do they have to carry the can when pastoral disasters follow bad appointments.

All this leads some people to question the validity of the patron's role in the modern church. That is an understandable but mistaken reaction, though patrons who sit back on their legal rights without any regard for the others involved in the process deserve all the criticism they get.

There is still, in fact, a pressing need for a third party to be involved (in addition to the bishop and the PCC) when a new vicar or rector is appointed. In times when financial crises can so easily dominate ecclesiastical practice, the local church may well need a powerful ally to counter its bishop's tendency to play 'diocesan chess' by pressing the claims of an unsuitable candidate who has to be moved from elsewhere. And bishops sometimes welcome allies too, especially when powerful churches 'go congregational' and try to insist on recruiting their own vicars on the 'he who pays the piper calls the tune' principle.

Apart from acting as honest brokers, modern patrons can also make a positive contribution in other valuable ways. Scandalous stories about private patrons who have no Christian faith and/or seek to exercise their rights long after their ties with the local communities they represent have been broken can easily be countered by examples of men and women who are long-standing members of their congregations and bring a wealth of local knowledge to the process of finding a new vicar. And patronage trusts, though geographically more distant, have a corporate knowledge of potential candidates which dwarfs the combined resources of diocese and PCC.

Patronage trustees would add that the primary reason for the establishment of the trusts they serve is more than an anachronistic curiosity. Experience elsewhere in the Anglican Communion, where patronage does not exist, suggests that distinctive traditions can gradually be marginalized in dioceses where they are not valued.

The PCC and its Representatives - *spiritually discerning people.*

One important feature of the 1986 Measure is that the local church's PCC has a more effective say in the appointments process. That is expressed partly in the statement about the parish's needs which the whole PCC must agree and own (see below), and partly by the election of two members to represent it in the negotiations which follow.

Previously, the churchwardens were allowed to object to a candidate's appointment. Nowadays, the PCC's elected representatives (who may or may not be the wardens) must be consulted and give their agreement before an appointment can be made. If just one of them responds negatively, the veto on the patron's nominee can only be overturned by an appeal to the archbishop. That right of appeal is very rarely exercised. It is likely, of course, that the candidate would withdraw anyway in the face of such strong opposition.

Patrons and bishops sometimes complain that PCC representatives do not understand the limits of their role. That may, of course, simply be an expression of frustration when the appointment of a preferred candidate is legitimately blocked.

Any 'misunderstanding' may also express the representatives' frustration, felt all the more keenly if they are professionally involved in making secular appointments, when they discover that all they are really allowed to do is to say 'yes' or 'no.' The law effectively distances them from the earlier part of the process when candidates are short-listed and selected. That can be particularly irritating if the PCC has been asked to pay for an advertisement and its representatives are then prevented from seeing the details of those who apply.

The law does not lay down any ground rules for the way PCC representatives are meant to make up their minds. Here there is room for a great deal of local initiative and flexibility which may draw frowns or applause from different bishops and patrons. Some suggestions are made below, in the section on 'good practice,' but it is ultimately up to the representatives themselves to decide how they go about their legitimate business.

Their power of veto should not be mis-represented as a negative irritant in the process. When representatives say 'no' to a nominee they are expressing their uniquely intimate knowledge of their own church and community. In effect they are saying, 'The Revd Pat Bloggs may be an excellent person, but he or she is not right for us here.' That is an entirely positive contribution. It helps patrons fine-tune their understanding of local needs as the process moves into its next phase.

When representatives say 'no' to a nominee they are expressing their uniquely intimate knowledge of their own church and community

The Bishop—and the Archbishop

By virtue of his office, the bishop may veto the patron's nomination (subject, again, to a right of appeal to the archbishop). If he approves, he seals the appointment by instituting the nominee—and, of course, thereby accepts responsibility for the instituted incumbent from that point on.

Sometimes the bishop is also the patron, so the 'tripod of responsibility' loses one of its legs. The PCC representatives may consequently come under considerable episcopal pressure to accept the diocese's preferred candidate.

We believe that bishops may sometimes be too proactive when they do not hold or share patronage responsibilities. PCCs may be given the impression that the diocese is in the driving seat when it comes to appointing a vicar's successor. Patrons may be informed that they can only begin a search for candidates outside the diocese when an internal search by the bishop and his staff has been exhausted. Episcopally chaired patronage boards are sometimes not convened until the process has reached a point where candidates have been gathered and—occasionally—short-listed. In our opinion, such practices are wrong. We are not saying that they represent a deliberate attempt to hijack the system. They are often understandable responses to financial pressures or even expressions of a desire to get ponderous machinery moving quickly (with which the parish concerned may strongly sympathize). But they do threaten the stability of the 'tripod' and sometimes strain crucial relationships.

As the church's accredited leaders, bishops do, of course, have a vital role to play in appointing clergy. After all, it is they who have to pick up the pieces after a disastrous appointment. As we make clear in the section below on 'good practice,' we do not believe that bishops should be left standing isolated on the touchline until patrons have nominees whom PCC representatives have approved. The collaborative spirit in which all concerned should be seeking to discern God's will demands that the bishop should be fully involved from beginning to end of the process.

Apart from hearing rare appeals from patrons and bishops (and, of course, acting in his diocesan capacity), there is another point in the process where the archbishop of the province may get involved.

Under section 16 of the 1986 <u>Measure</u> a patron has up to nine months to make a presentation to a benefice. When that period expires, the right of presentation lapses to the archbishop. If explorations with a candidate are at an intermediate stage they may be allowed to proceed, but that cannot be automatically assumed. The PCC representatives also lose their right of veto.

In cases of lapse, the usual practice is for the archbishop to ask the diocesan bishop to lead the search for a suitable incumbent. On the diocese's advice the archbishop will then consider a candidate in the light of the PCC's statement about the parish's needs.

This is clearly good practice (in that the diocese will have superior local knowledge) but it does have the effect of bringing the bishop back onto centre stage while the patron remains in the wings. It may be appropriate for the bishop to consult the patron more fully than the letter of the law requires, especially when the lapse has occurred for reasons other than unreasonable delay on the patron's part. Some patrons complain the Measure's time constraints are too tight, especially when multi-parish benefices are involved.

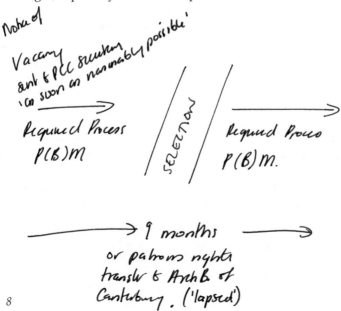

Models of the Process at Work 3

Although the Patronage (Benefices) Measure sets out the parameters within which procedures for appointing a new vicar or rector must take place, it leaves plenty of space inside the fences within which individual patrons, trusts and patronage boards can legitimately operate. Practices inevitably vary, and that may lead to confusion and puzzlement.

Here are four of the more usual modes of operation. All are valid, and each has its staunch advocates. There are, of course, equally cogent variations of all four.

Presentation Model *Is this what happened in B'sea? This is not @ competition but discernment.*

In this model of the process the patron will present just one candidate for the PCC representatives to approve. In its extreme form there will have been no consultation beforehand and no explanatory papers (such as a CV) will precede the candidate's arrival. He or she will have been selected by the patron after consulting with trusted contacts. The PCC representatives will be deterred from taking up references and laying on rigorous interviews. The assumption is that the patron's decision should be accepted as final without too many questions asked.

Consultation Model *CPAS*

Patrons who operate in the 'consultation' mode make it clear from the outset that they reserve the right to decide (subject to the PCC representatives' veto) who shall eventually be nominated to the bishop. Nevertheless, they are careful to consult their partners in the process. Bishops are asked for names—but without any guarantee that one of them will appear on the short list. Representatives may be asked to meet two or three candidates—but are firmly reminded that it is not their right to make a choice.

Joint Interview Model *Becoming hugely popular.*

This method culminates in an 'interview day,' when patron, PCC representatives and bishop meet a number of candidates and seek a common mind on their suitability. At the beginning of the process the vacancy is usually advertised (advertising can also feature, of course, in the other three models), so that all three parties are free to prompt likely candidates to apply. The patron normally assumes responsibility for deciding which applicants are to be interviewed, sometimes after consultation with the bishop. The assumption is that God's will becomes more clear when candidates are closely compared. The competitive edge is softened by an attempt to immerse the process in a prayerful desire on everyone's part to discern the person whom God wants appointed.

Collaboration Model *can be a fudge. Prove to Bishops driving it. People who suffer = clergy.*

Patrons who work this way sit light to the distinctions between the legal responsibilities of the three parties involved. They strive to make the process totally open and highly visible from start to finish. Bishops are invited to submit names and PCC representatives are involved with them in short-listing candidates. Unanimity is sought before a final decision is reached — so the legalities become a formality. The model may be summed up in the phrase, 'Let us work this out together.'

✱ in multi-parish situations v. complicated.
Former patronage rights ⇒ patronage board.

Suspension

4

Everything we have written so far assumes that the process set in place by the Measure of 1986 is allowed to take its course without a hitch.

There are situations, however, in which the bishop is entitled (under section 67 or 69 of the Pastoral Measure 1983) to build a delay into the system. By s67, with the consent of the Diocesan Pastoral Committee, he is allowed to *suspend* the patron's right to present a nominee for a vacant benefice in certain circumstances for a maximum perioed of five years. Before doing so he must consult all the interested parties. This may be done for a number of reasons.

First, and most often, he may suspend the process of appointing an incumbent while a Pastoral Scheme affecting the benefice passes through its various consultative stages. Such a Scheme often involves joining two or more benefices into a group, a team or a new united benefice. Bishops are prone to suspend whenever there is a possibility of future pastoral reorganization of this kind taking place. It is not clear how far the discussions should have progressed before a bishop is justified in suspending the presentation. In practice the power is used very freely, perhaps too freely.

Secondly, suspension is allowed when the bishop wants to change the parsonage house of a benefice. If there is an incumbent in office, a change of vicarage or rectory can only happen with his or her consent, so it is common practice to delay taking action until there is a vacancy. Suspension creates enough space, before the next incumbent moves in, for the necessary arrangements to be made.

Thirdly, suspensions sometimes occur when an incoming parish priest will be required to take on additional diocesan responsibilities. In theory, a clergyperson in this position—if instituted with a freehold—could abandon the 'sector ministry' and then successfully resist all attempts to remove him or her from the parish. Suspension is used as a device to stop that happening.

By s69(2) the bishop may *restrict* the patron's right to present for a period of one year, where pastoral reorganization is *already* under formal discussion. The main distinction here is that this can be done without consultation, but only for the shorter period. It seems clearer in this section of the measure that formal proposals for reorganization should be under way before the section is used by the bishop.

Suspension or restriction of the patron's right to present does not mean that the parish cannot have a minister. Instead of a vicar or rector the bishop may appoint a priest-in-charge. The latter is licensed for a period, not instituted with a freehold, but he or she is usually accepted by the parish as 'the vicar.'

The difference in the appointment of a priest-in-charge is that the bishop is not bound to accept the patron's suggestions or to respect the PCC's objections. In the authors' experience, episcopal practice varies enormously in these situations between the extremes of full consultation and thinly veiled autocracy. More will be said about this in the chapter on 'good practice.'

Suspension and restriction mean exactly what they say. They are not creating an alternative system of making appointments but are a temporary interruption of the process set out in the Patronage (Benefices) Measure. A suspension order may be renewed, but bishops should expect searching questions to be asked by the PCC and patron when re-suspension is proposed. (If the original order anticipated pastoral reorganization, for example, why has this not yet taken place?) If, as is beginning to happen, proposals are made to extend suspension for a third five year period, bishops must not be surprised if patrons and PCCs begin to suspect abuse. These suspicions will be allayed to a great extent, of course, if bishops consult fully and openly with the other parties involved whenever suspension is contemplated. If a priest-in-charge is in office when suspension or restriction is lifted the patron and PCC representatives have complete freedom to decide whether or not to nominate and affirm him or her as the incumbent. This makes it all the more sensible for bishops to consult fully before imposing suspension in the first place.

The Key Steps in Making an Appointment

5

Assuming there is to be no suspension of the patron's rights (or whenever the suspension is lifted), the following are the main steps which need to be taken in appointing a vicar or a rector. A fuller version is set out in Appendix 3.

Getting Started

Register in BFs [handwritten annotation]

When an incumbent resigns, retires or dies the bishop is notified of the impending vacancy. He, in turn, notifies the diocese's 'Designated Officer,' who informs the registered patron(s). Patrons are required to return a form stating whether they intend to carry out their duties themselves or appoint others to act on their behalf. Anyone who fills the patron's role must sign a declaration that he or she is a communicant member of the Church of England or of a church which is in communion with it.

The Designated Officer also notifies the secretary of the PCC(s). It (or they) must meet within 28 days to discuss and decide six matters which the Notice of Vacancy specifies. In the case of multi-parish benefices the PCCs have to meet together to take these decisions.

Here are the six things the PCC(s) must do. The first five are listed in section 11(1) of the Patronage (Benefices) Measure. The sixth arises from the legislation allowing the ordination of women.

PARISH PROFILE - lengthy @ chg. VISION FOR FUTURE + PERSON SPEC. Tell you what is going on. [handwritten annotation]

is v. different to the Profile. [handwritten annotation, left margin]

(a) ***Prepare a statement describing the conditions, needs and traditions of the parish.*** This is a crucial document. As well as the essential factual information, it should contain the PCC's estimate of the qualities and skills required in the next vicar or rector. Many dioceses provide guidelines or a *pro forma* to help PCCs in this task. Once completed, copies of the statement must be sent, within strict time limits, to both patron and bishop. If more than one parish is involved, a joint statement may be produced. Alternatively, different parishes may make separate statements—in which case a coordinating addendum is very helpful.

(b) ***Appoint two lay members to represent the PCC in the process.*** They may, but need not, be the churchwardens. It is these representatives who have the power to approve the patron's nominee. When more than one PCC is involved each council has the right to elect at least one member to represent it. The Code of Practice issued in 1989 suggests the following pattern:

2 parishes: 2 representatives from each PCC
3 parishes: either 2 from each or 2 from one and 1 from each of the other two
4 or more parishes: 1 from each

(c) *Decide whether to request the patron(s) to advertise the post.* The PCC cannot insist, and it may well be expected to foot the bill if the patron agrees. 2006 -happened in B'ham.

(d) *Decide whether to ask for a meeting of bishop, patron and PCC to discuss the parish statement.* Any of the three parties may call for such a meeting under section 12 of the Measure, which is why it is usually called a Section 12 meeting. Bishops vary greatly in the way they use this right. Some call Section 12 meetings as a matter of course, while others regard them as emergency fall-back devices only to be used when relationships are particularly fragile and misunderstandings likely.

(e) *Decide whether to request a statement in writing from the bishop describing the needs of the diocese in relation to the benefice and the wider interests of the church.* Most PCCs feel this is an unnecessary step if the bishop or archdeacon is planning to visit them anyway in order to discuss the vacancy. If, however, the bishop expects the incumbent of a small benefice to take on additional diocesan duties it may help the PCC and patron to have some firm information about the level of commitment involved.

(f) *Consider two formal resolutions arising from the Priests (Ordination of Women) Measure 1993.* These are:

Resolution A
That this PCC would not accept a woman as the minister who presides at or celebrates Holy Communion or pronounces Absolution in this parish.

Resolution B
That this PCC would not accept a woman as Incumbent or Priest-in-Charge of the benefice or as a Team Vicar in the benefice.

The PCC is not required to vote on either resolution if it does not want to, but it is required to decide whether to vote or not. Its representatives are open to prosecution if they veto the appointment of a woman (on gender grounds alone) when Resolution B has not been passed.

It is the PCC's responsibility, then, to take the most important steps in initiating the process for appointing a new vicar or rector. Inevitably, it takes time and effort to do all these things well. So much the better, therefore, if the outgoing incumbent can give the PCC a little notice of his or her intention to go so that it can push ahead with its preparations before the Measure's deadlines become operative. This is particularly valuable for multi-parish benefices where timetabling meetings and setting up the necessary structures for liaison may be time-consuming.

Gathering Names

This is the patron's primary contribution to the process. In whatever way patronage is expressed (through an individual, a group, a trust or a board) the initial aim is to find a number of ordained men—and women (unless the PCC has passed Resolution B)—who most closely match the situation, tasks and needs identified by the parish statement.

Patrons have a number of resources to help them in this exercise. Mercifully, the caricature of a private patron scratching his head and doing his best to remember which clergymen he can recall whose sermons have bored him least is a thing of the past. Whether individuals or groups, modern patrons can tap into various networks to provide them with suitable names. The wisdom of the diocesan staff meeting can always be accessed through the bishop. The Clergy Appointments Adviser (see Appendix 4) will also be glad to help with more names from outside the diocese. If someone of evangelical persuasion would suit the vacancy, the Evangelical Patrons Consultative Council (EPCC) keeps a register of clergy who are seeking moves. That is administered by the Patronage Secretary of the Church Pastoral Aid Society (CPAS) and its resources are always available to patrons of non-CPAS livings.

Patronage trusts are especially well placed in this hunt for suitable candidates. A major criterion for the selection of trustees is normally a greater-than-usual knowledge of clergy across the country. Most of the larger trusts meet between six and twelve times annually to consider names for the vacancies on their list, and the corporate wisdom expressed around the table at those meetings is impressive. Several trusts have computer databases to aid fallible memories and to avoid the hazards of the 'old boy network.'

Then, of course, there is always the possibility of advertising the vacancy in the church press. An advertisement may prompt a good candidate whose name is not on anyone's list.

What patrons do with the names they collect will vary according to their different modes of operation (as outlined in the chapter on 'Models of the Process at Work' above). Some will send their single 'best choice' for the PCC representatives to approve. Others will offer the top three candidates on their short lists to the representatives. Others again will set up an 'interview day' in which a number of candidates will be seen. And before any of that is done, some patrons will send their short-listed names to the bishop for his clearance.

At the end of the day, the patron has to narrow the choice to just one person, whose name is sent to the bishop with the request that he or she should be instituted as incumbent of the vacant benefice.

Approving the Candidate(s)

Legally, this is the prerogative of the elected PCC representatives. Indeed, their only formal role is to decide whether or not they wish to approve the patron's nomination.

Some patrons will seek to involve them much more than that (see again the section above on 'Models of the Process at Work'), but the representatives can only take a fuller part in the process if the patron invites them to do so. If he or she does not, they have no formal grounds for complaint—even if a vacancy in a neighbouring parish has been handled very differently.

They will, of course, have a perfectly legitimate concern to maximize their information about any candidate before deciding whether or not to approve him or her. Some patrons will provide plenty of paperwork in advance of the candidate's visit, but others will not. There are various options open to the PCC representatives at this point (see the section on 'Good Practice' below). They may seek the help of others, but they must remember that the final decision is theirs and theirs alone.

If they decide to veto the patron's nominee, and the patron does not appeal against their decision to the archbishop, the process simply moves back a step and the patron puts forward another candidate.

Completing the Appointment

Both the PCC representatives and the bishop have to sign legal documents accepting the patron's nomination. If the bishop has not been brought into the process before this stage, he will almost certainly want to interview the chosen candidate himself before signing on the dotted line.

Once the documents have been signed the patron can formally offer the benefice to the priest. The priest must reply accepting the post. The patron then gives notice of presentation to the bishop. It is only at this point that a public announcement can be made—preferably in both the candidate's and the 'receiving' church on the same Sunday—and a date fixed for the new incumbent's institution and induction.

The bishop will do the instituting (giving the priest permission to minister) and the archdeacon the inducting (giving the priest the legal ownership of parochial property). The vocabulary can be rather perplexing! 'Institution' becomes 'collation' when the bishop is also the patron. And if the appointment is that of priest-in-charge (following suspension) the bishop's part of the ceremony is called 'licensing' and the archdeacon's 'installation.'

Even at this stage, when the date of the institution (or whatever) has been fixed, the legalities are not quite complete. The bishop must give formal notice to the designated officer, the registrar, the patron, the archdeacon, the rural dean and the incumbent-to-be. The registrar then notifies the PCC secretary, who is instructed to post a notice on the church door for a fortnight announcing the bishop's intention to institute a new incumbent. Only when this notice has been sent back to the registrar with the PCC secretary's endorsement can the institution proceed.

The process is complete. The local church can now give thanks to God, as it embarks on a new phase of its life.

Good Practice 6

This section reflects the authors' own preferences. It should be read in that light. Some will agree with the general thrust of the collaborative style it encourages without being able to agree with every detail of the strategy it advocates. Others will conclude that we have been far too cautious. Much of what we suggest has either been included in the Patronage (Benefices) Measure Code of Conduct or has already been adopted as standard practice by particular dioceses or patrons.

If we were producing a contribution to the internet, this would be the point where the whole exercise becomes interactive. We would certainly welcome comments and criticisms anyway, because all the parties involved in appointing new incumbents are searching for new and better ways of making their methods more user-friendly and honouring to God.

In days when the church has rediscovered the virtues of collaborative ministry, good practice in making appointments to local church leadership ought surely to be marked by good, open, cooperative relationships between all who are involved in the process. At various points the law requires the main parties to consult. But consultation—like justice—must not only be done but seen to be done. To put it negatively, in most cases where one party or another feels the process has been badly handled it is because the aggrieved member of the partnership feels marginalized or misunderstood.

This points to one solid advantage of the provision for a meeting between PCC, patron and diocesan representatives under section 12 of the Measure (see the section above on 'The Key Steps'). If a section 12 meeting is perceived as a 'last hope' safety net, only to be used when relationships are already tearing apart at the seams, there will be an understandable reluctance ever to call one. But if such a meeting is seen as a golden opportunity to gather the three key players under one roof at the same time to discuss with the whole PCC the details of the parish statement (which is the only item allowed on the agenda), the gain in terms of mutual understanding and confidence is potentially great.

If a section 12 meeting is perceived as a 'last hope' safety net, there will be an understandable reluctance ever to call one

We set out below some thoughts as to how each of the three parties involved can go about exercising their rights and responsibilities under the Measure. However, before addressing each party separately there is one further piece of advice worth giving. As we point out elsewhere (Chapter 3: Models of the Process at Work) the way in which the legislation is applied in each vacancy can validly vary. We suggest that it is to everyone's advantage for the patron, bishop and parish representatives to have a conversation very early in the vacancy as to how the whole process will be handled. Who will decide when candidates visit the parish and who will they meet when they get there? Will there be interviews involving the bishop, patron and parish representatives, or will the patron want to make a selection before candidates are offered to the parish representatives and the bishop? If there is clarity as to how the process will be handled those with least experience in these matters (the parish representatives and the candidates) are more likely to feel the process is open and equitable.

Bishops

Bishops are used to operating collaboratively within their own diocesan structures. Vacancies are normally discussed at regular staff meetings attended by archdeacons as well as by diocesan and area bishops. It is perfectly normal practice for a bishop to delegate to an archdeacon some of his responsibilities during the earlier stages of appointing a new vicar or rector, so a parish should not feel itself short-changed or demeaned if the PCC is approached by the archdeacon initially. Communications between archdeacon and bishop are personal, open and frequent.

A parish should not feel itself short-changed or demeaned if the PCC is approached by the archdeacon initially

Bishops are pastorally responsible for parochial clergy, so it is only natural that they should want a major role in appointing them. It is not at all clear, however, where such a legitimate concern becomes over-directive in a process which is intended to be genuinely tripartite. For example, we would question the advisability of advertising a vacancy in a diocesan hand-out before patrons are informed about it. And the natural desire to manage the parochial end of the process by getting diocesan officers to chair PCC meetings where the parish profile is put together and—further down the line—other meetings where PCC representatives interview candidates, can easily become more heavy than helpful.

The main pressure points here are the management of *team ministries* and the appointment of *priests-in-charge*, because in both these cases the bishop is given extra powers which may undermine the rights of PCCs and patrons.

When a *team ministry* is created, patronage passes into the hands of the Diocesan Board of Patronage or, more usually, a special patronage board (unless the bishop was formerly the sole patron, in which case he may choose to retain his rights—an odd anomaly). In the vast majority of cases, the bishop becomes *ex officio* chairman of the patronage board, often with a casting vote. Former sole patrons sometimes find themselves on the board with minority voting rights only, which seems to us manifestly unjust.

Normally the PCC and existing members of the parochial staff are also represented. Their inclusion at the stage of choice certainly brings a fresh collaborative flavour into the process, though it can also muddy the waters (in that the PCC may appoint two other representatives to exercise its statutory right of veto).

The real winner, however, is the diocese—especially as the archdeacon is usually on the board as well as the bishop. In these circumstances good practice demands that the bishop should use his role as chairman with enormous care, to ensure that the process is genuinely collaborative and not subliminally driven from the diocesan centre.

When a bishop decides to suspend the patron's rights he cannot appoint a new vicar or rector, but he may (and usually does) license a *priest-in-charge* to take care of the parish(es) concerned. Regrettably, these appointments are sometimes made after a minimum of consultation with the patron and PCC (which loses its right of veto just as the patron loses his right to nominate). In other cases the bishop lets both PCC and patron know at the very beginning of the process that it is his intention to involve them as fully as they would be in the appointment of an incumbent. We believe the latter approach constitutes good practice. Given the need to suspend (for any of the three reasons already mentioned), there seems no cogent reason why the patron and PCC representatives should be prevented from taking their full part in the process of finding a suitable candidate for the bishop to license.

Patrons

Legally, a patron may dominate the appointment process. He or she can decline any assistance in identifying good candidates, refuse the PCC's request to advertise the vacancy, send a nominee (just one) to the PCC representatives without any supporting information, and choose not to bring the bishop into the picture until the very last moment.[2]

We do not regard this as good practice. Patrons, in our view, should take the initiative in seeking fresh ways and means of bringing both bishops and PCCs into the heart of the process. We realize, however, that this requires great care and involves some risk if the edges of the patrons' own responsibility are not to be blurred.

Good practice requires open communication between patron and bishop. Asking the bishop's staff meeting for good diocesan names and referring shortlists to bishops for comment before candidates are approached seem obvious ways of cementing this important relationship. The patron's integrity is only threatened if one name is pressed too strongly or if the shortlist comes back with the candidates renumbered. Both are relatively small risks to take, as each can be resisted.

Good practice calls for open lines of communication between patron and parish

Similarly, good practice calls for open lines of communication between patron and parish. Patrons are unlikely to find their names in the 'good patron guide' if they make no contact with their parishes between vacancies. As soon as the vacancy is notified, a good patron will want to visit the PCC, in order to gain full, accurate information about the parish's present needs.[3] This consultative exercise is even more important when the patron (a trust, perhaps, or an Oxbridge college) is geographically distant from the local scene. Questions will need to be asked about the contents of the parish profile and the PCC's stated requirements of its next vicar or rector if a clear, detailed picture is to emerge.

Some patrons will want to involve PCCs much more fully than that as the process unfolds. Should PCC representatives be allowed to meet a number of candidates, rather than just one at a time? And if so, how should the process be managed—by an 'interview day' when all concerned (including the candidates and the bishop) work collaboratively to discern the person of God's choice, or by some other means? Should a good patron positively encourage a PCC to request advertisement of the vacancy? After all, God may use an advert to prompt an excellent candidate whose name is not on anyone's list! And if the PCC foots the bill for the advertising, should the patron allow its elected representatives to see some, most or all of the application papers—before, during or after candidates have been short listed?

In our view, good practice requires the patron to find convincing answers to questions like these, even though different answers may lead to a spectrum of legitimate approaches. There are, of course, variable factors to be taken into account as well, such as the patron's opinion about the efficacy of advertising, ability to deal with the paperwork that an advertisement may produce, desire to make procedures as simple as possible—or, indeed, the way his or her theology affects the process of appointing church leaders.

At the deeper level, a good patron will want to gain clear impressions at an early stage about the nature of the local church and the style of the ministry it expects. These are matters which become more important and much more complex when several communities and congregations are involved. Some typical models of the church and models of ministry are set out in Appendix 2. It would be interesting to get a PCC to describe itself and its aspirations by numbering the options on those lists in an order of priority. Certainly, if things go wrong after an appointment, the problem is far more likely to be located in the mismatched expectations of parish and priest than in any misunderstanding of the factual information recorded in the parish's profile or the priest's *curriculum vitae*.

PCC Representatives

The representatives' role is reactive but vital. Their right to affirm or veto the patron's nominee should certainly be seen as a highly positive contribution to the process as a whole.

To do their job well, they need good information. The patron who aims to work collaboratively will not send a candidate for interview without posting some supportive paperwork in advance. This should comprise a full CV at the very least. If an application form has been used, it should be made clear to applicants that copies of this, too, will be forwarded to the PCC representatives. Some patrons also ask candidates for brief, specific responses to the parish profile and those can be very helpful guides in setting up an interview agenda.

Representatives may also want to take up references. Some patrons regard this as rather 'over the top,' while others ask referees' permission to send copies of their comments on candidates to parishes as a matter of course. We regard it as good practice for representatives to seek the confidential opinions of third parties about anyone they are asked to interview, whatever arrangements may or may not be in place for the sharing of such information.

Once a candidate's details are known, some representatives welcome the opportunity to see him or her in action. This may be particularly important if preaching and leading of worship are considered vital skills in the new vicar's profile. Good practice suggests, however, that the candidate is carefully consulted before an exploratory visit to his or her present church is made. Some vicars and curates have excellent reasons for *not* wanting their congregations to know that they are contemplating a move, and it can be highly embarrassing if the investigators' disguises and alibis are penetrated—which on these occasions they often are.

Some representatives find their role too hard to bear alone. How, they ask, can they be sure that they are representing their PCCs fairly, rather than expressing their own preferences? Those who have elected them sometimes share their misgivings and appoint sub-committees to help (and monitor) them in their work.

If this 'support' goes very much further than a pledge of prayer, we believe it may be misguided. Election means empowerment. Representatives must be trusted as well as chosen. This is not to suggest, of course, that candidates should be prevented from seeing anyone else when they visit the parish, nor to pretend that it is in some way unethical for those they meet to voice an opinion. In churches where there are already fully developed ministry teams it is obviously vital for candidates to meet those with whom they may share the responsibilities of leadership. Nevertheless, good practice demands that PCCs' elected representatives should be allowed to make their decisions without undue pressure from others.

It is also good practice to give candidates time and space to ask their own questions when they come for interview. And as they are seeking God's will just as much as everyone else in the process, they will probably welcome the freedom to walk a few streets and pray in the church on their own as well as being taken on conducted tours.

The Candidate's Angle 7

The contents of this booklet mainly concern the three parties who have the statutory right under the Patronage (Benefices) Measure to appoint new incumbents to vacant benefices. But there is, of course, a fourth party without whom the whole process could not go anywhere. It is by no means uncommon for the patron, the bishop and the PCC representatives to be in complete agreement about a candidate's suitability—only for the candidate himself or herself to withdraw.

How does an ordained person discern God's will in the process, once begun?

How does an ordained person go about finding a new post, if that job entails institution as an incumbent or licensing as a priest-in-charge? And how, apart from prayer, does he or she discern God's will in the process, once begun?

Thirty years ago it was not uncommon to find clergy who believed that the right thing to do, when contemplating a move, was to sit back and wait for an approach to come. To take the initiative by expressing a personal interest in a particular vacancy was considered arrogant. To respond to an advertisement in the church press would be to set an obstacle in the path of the Holy Spirit's guidance. And to put your name on the Church Appointments Adviser's list would be a sign of desperation.

In case somebody has not yet noticed, times have changed dramatically! Those who restrict their search to straightforward single-church incumbencies will find their options severely limited by the creation of team ministries, the uniting of benefices and the proliferation of suspension. It is now commonplace (though expensive) for vacancies to be advertised in the church press; and the 'interview day', when several candidates are invited to participate in the selection process, is fast becoming the norm instead of the exception. Clergy who decide not to be proactive in making their availability known may face a long and frustrating wait.

Other factors contribute to the complexity of the situation. Clergy who look for a move in their late fifties or early sixties will discover that ageism lurks between the lines in many parish profiles. And those trying to return from posts overseas may find it hard to decide whether or not to apply for jobs which require interviews on dates which do not easily fit into a single visit to the UK.

All is not doom and gloom by any means. Many clergy welcome the increasing openness in the process as a channel through which God can sharpen their perception of his calling. But the difficulties some face should not be underestimated. It is certainly not faithless to be proactive.

Taking the following practical steps will often help.

Networking

Make sure that your availability is widely known. First and foremost, let your bishop and archdeacon know that you are considering a move. This is especially helpful if you are open to a move within a diocese, as financial pressures predispose bishops to consider diocesan candidates first. But informing your present bishop of your intentions is a sensible thing to do anyway, because the bishop of any diocese in which you are seeking a new post will undoubtedly approach him for a reference before agreeing to institute you. He will, of course, be pastorally concerned for you as well, as you seek God's will for your future ministry.

Next, consider having your name added to either or both of the lists regularly used by patrons. These are the Clergy Appointments Adviser's list and (if you are an evangelical) the Evangelical Patrons Consultative Council's register, which is administered by the Church Pastoral Aid Society's patronage secretary. Getting on to either will involve some form-filling, when you can state your preferences, and an interview, when these choices can be fine-tuned and better understood.

It is probably best (again, if you are an evangelical) to have your name on both lists. Though each is available to any patron who requests it, bishops tend to work primarily from the CAA list and patronage trusts look first to the EPCC register. You can usefully supplement both exercises by writing, with your *curriculum vitae*, to the secretaries of suitable patronage trusts individually, and to the person responsible for finding candidates for benefices belonging to the Crown's or Lord Chancellor's patronage. His details are in Appendix 4.

Finally, as part of the 'networking' exercise, consult the advertisement pages of the church press (the *Church Times* and the *Church of England Newspaper*) regularly. And never assume that a patron who advertises will automatically think of you if he knows about your availability already. If you do not apply, he will probably assume that you are not interested in the advertised post.

Flexibility

Sooner or later (and certainly at your CAA or CPAS interview) you will be asked how widely you are prepared to set your fences. It is sensible, therefore, to think and pray carefully beforehand about the limits you mean to impose.

And naturally the fewer fences you set up, the more will be the opportunities you are asked to consider.

When you are invited to express geographical preferences, remember—before you rule anything out—that (for example) East Anglia includes Cambridge and Ipswich as well as remote rural communities; and that the Midlands comprise rural Leicestershire and Northamptonshire as well as major industrial conurbations like Birmingham and Coventry. Remember, too, that the term 'Urban Priority Area' embraces a spectrum of social settings, some of which may suit your style of ministry more than others. And if family circumstances (ageing parents, perhaps) rule some places out of bounds, think practically about travelling time rather than of distance alone.

Remember that the term 'Urban Priority Area' embraces a spectrum of social settings

You should also carefully consider how far (if at all) you are prepared to work beyond the confines of your own tradition. If you are an evangelical, would you be prepared to look at a parish where the profile insists that you sometimes wear full vestments but offers you complete freedom to preach the gospel and teach biblically?

This kind of decision becomes vital when a multi-church vacancy comes into view. Almost inevitably, whether or not you are an acceptable candidate will depend on your willingness to be flexible. How far can you adapt your practice before you compromise your theology or spoil your integrity? Whatever the shape of your answer, the question is certainly worth pondering before you decide whether this kind of opening is right for you or not.

Paperwork and Interviews

One diocesan bishop avoids 'interview days' like the plague because he fears that only clergy who thrive in competitive situations will succeed. Some applicants share his anxieties. Nevertheless, any candidate for an incumbency post today must expect to be interviewed rigorously at some point in the process, whether the patron favours 'interview days' or not.

It therefore makes excellent sense to ensure, as far as you can, that you do yourself justice in an interview situation. In the context of an appointment to a church the intention is not, of course, to pull wool over the questioners' eyes. But it is a great help to them, not least in discerning God's will, if you hear their questions accurately and answer them clearly and fully. To do their job well, they need an accurate picture of your qualities and gifts, not a foggy impression glimpsed through the mist of inadequate self-presentation. The message is clear—if you are not good at being interviewed, seek some appropriate help now.

Much the same can be said about the paperwork that is usually required of applicants today. If a patron receives twenty application forms, and yours is the only one filled in shoddily and inadequately (because you are too busy to give it much attention), you may be creating an unnecessary obstacle. It is certainly unlikely that your name will appear on the shortlist. To put the same thing more positively, a morning spent on producing a full and accurate *curriculum vitae* is time well spent if you seriously believe God is calling you to make a move.

Choose your referees with care as well. Avoid the ultra-busy who will not have time to aim their references specifically at the job(s) for which you are applying. And do not steer clear of those who will write as frankly about your weaknesses as they do about your strengths. Patrons (and parishes!) warm to honesty and distrust references that appear to describe the archangel Gabriel.

8

Conclusion

A necessary final word! Some of the advice in this booklet may sound very secular in its tone, even though it is offered in the hope that it will remove obstacles in the way of discerning God's will.

Discovering what God wants is, of course, the whole aim of the exercise. Within that framework no-one really has any *choices* to make. Just as a vicar's departure does not take God by surprise, so the selection of his or her successor is something God has already arranged. The primary responsibility of those who are involved in the appointment process is to avoid making mistakes and perceive his will accurately. Only then will the church receive a new leader with a compelling call and a clear vision to take it forward in God's way.

Ultimately, God can work outside ecclesiastical structures as well as within them. Many are the examples of right appointments being made when the people concerned have made all the 'wrong' approaches. That is certainly comforting—but equally certainly not an excuse to by-pass the care and hard work that is needed to get things right.

Appendix 1:
Models of Pastoral Organization

Benefices are established in a wide variety of ways, according to the history of a place and the reasons for the reorganization. This list describes the most common forms of organization.

1   *Single Parish:* One parish with one church, one PCC and one incumbent, and possibly with assistant clergy.

2   *United Parish:* Several communities with one or more churches, one PCC and one incumbent, and possibly with assistant clergy.

3   *United Benefice:* Several parishes with several churches, several PCCs and one incumbent, and possibly with assistant clergy.

4   *Team Ministry:* Several communities with several churches, but with one PCC and one incumbent, with assistant clergy.

5   *Group Ministry:* Several parishes with several churches, several PCCs and several incumbents (being committed to work together), possibly with assistant clergy.

6   *Plurality:* Several parishes with several churches and several PCCs, but with one person as incumbent of all of the benefices.

7   *Priest-in-Charge:* Any of the above models but without the senior priest being the incumbent.

The patronage of a benefice may vary according to the pastoral organization of that benefice. In the case of model 1 the patron is usually a sole patron, either an individual, an office holder or a body corporate. In the case of models 2, 3, 5 & 6 the historic patrons of each parish are usually represented. This may mean that they take turns to appoint, or that they work jointly or that they are formed into a patronage board with each historic patron having a vote. In the case of model 4 it is usual for there to be a team patronage board, which may contain representatives of the historic patrons of each parish, the diocese and the PCC. In model 7, of course, the patronage will depend on whatever model was in force before the suspension. The patron's rights of presentation are suspended but the patron must be consulted as to the appointment and should in our view be consulted as to suitable candidates for the post of Priest-in-Charge.

Appendix 2:
Models of Ministry and of the Church

As a PCC, it is vital to spend some quality time establishing your priorities when you draw up the 'person profile' for your new minister. This will enable you to identify which of the following models of ministry best represents your church(es) needs now. Communicating this clearly to candidates will assist the discernment process both for you and for them.

These models are not, of course, mutually exclusive. But do try to be realistic —not all the skills can be found in one human skin!

Models of Ministry

- *The Consultant:* Our priest should be a competent and skilled worker through whom people's experiences are interpreted.

- *The Overseer:* Our priest stands aside from the day-to-day life of others and gives some sense of oversight, like a watchman or a shepherd.

- *The Competent Professional:* Our priest should be one who has specialized skills and knowledge, and the ability to apply and communicate them.

- *The Practical Theologian:* Our priest should be a practical leader and a theological thinker giving vision and leadership, while enabling others to think theologically for themselves.

- *The Minister-in-Community:* Our priest should be but one part of the Christian community, enabling the formation of the whole community, and bringing the skills of others to the fore.

- *The Community Builder:* Our priest should be the person who builds a sense of community, especially through worship and pastoral care. This sense of community embraces the whole parish, not just the church congregation.

- *The Manager of Change:* Our priest should be a mediator of change, summed up in the biblical models of servant, shepherd, steward and overseer.

Models of the Church

- *The Institution:* We are part of the earthly institution that has Christ's authority to teach and to sanctify.
- *The Mystical Communion:* We are Christ's Body growing into perfection in the Kingdom of God.
- *The Sacrament:* We are the visible sign to the human race of God's grace in Christ.
- *The Herald:* We are those who have an authority to preach the divine message of the gospel to the world.
- *The Servant:* We are here for the service of the world and each other.
- *The Congregation:* We are God's people, responsible to one another before God.

A fuller consideration of the influence of these models is available in an unpublished work by David Parrott. The models themselves rely heavily on Avery Dulles, *Models of the Church* (Gill and Macmillan, 1987) and Ian Bunting, *Models of Ministry* (Grove Pastoral Series No 54, 1993).

Appendix 3: The 39 Steps

A Step-by-Step Guide to the Patronage (Benefices) Measure 1986

Step	Action	Form	Time Limit
1	The bishop is notified of a vacancy.		
2	Bishop gives notice of vacancy to Designated Officer		If on death, as soon as practicable. If on resignation, then such notice as bishop considers reasonable.
3	Designated Officer sends notice of vacancy to the registered patron	31	As soon as practicable after step 1.
4	Registered patron decides who will be the named representative of the patron to act in this case (especially in the case of a trust or collegiate body)		
5	Presenting patron sends to Designated Officer a declaration of actual communicant membership / ordination or names a representative to act who can make this declaration.	15 or 16	Within 2 months from step 3.

6	If patron fails to do so in time limit Designated Officer notifies bishop and patron that presentation has now lapsed to the diocesan bishop.		At end of two months from step 3.
7	On receipt of declaration in step 5 Designated Officer sends name and address of patron to PCC secretaries if necessary.	31, or 33	As soon as practicable.
8	Designated Officer sends notice of vacancy to secretary of each PCC involved.	31	As soon as practicable after step 3.
9	PCC secretaries call joint meeting of all PCCs involved to consider s11(1) agenda and resolutions under Priests (Ordination of Women) Measure 1993		Within 4 weeks of step 8.
10	PCC secretary sends to bishop and patron decisions of PCC in the six areas under step 9. NB If PCC secretary fails to send statement after a meeting held within 4 weeks then PCC representatives lose their right to refuse approval of priest chosen by patron under step 20.	34	As soon as practicable after step 9.
11	Patron may request s12 meeting	35	Within 10 days of receipt of step 10.
12	Bishop may request s12 meeting	35	Within 10 days of receipts of step 10.
13	Bishop sends statement if requested in step 9.		Within 10 days of receipt of step 10.
14	If a s12 meeting is requested by any of the parties then the PCC secretary must call a PCC meeting and give notice to PCC members, bishop, patron, Rural Dean and Lay Chairman of Deanery. The bishop and patron may each send a representative. NB If PCC secretary fails to convene a PCC within the period then the PCC loses its right to refuse approval of a candidate under step 20.		Meeting must be held within 6 weeks of either resolution at step 9 or of step 11 or 12. Notice of meeting must give 14 days notice.
15	s12 meeting is held.		
16	If no s12 meeting is requested then patron can proceed to step 17. If a s12 meeting is requested but is not called by the PCC secretary the patron cannot proceed as far as step 20 until 6 weeks from the notice, *ie* time limits in step 14 have passed.		
17	Patron selects a candidate. This can be by various methods—see main text.		None but note step 26 and its time limit.
18	Patron seeks approval for one candidate from bishop.	36	
19	Patron seeks approval for one candidate from PCC representatives.	37	
20	PCC representatives give approval to patron for his chosen candidate (go to step 24) or refuses approval (go to step 22).		Within 2 weeks of request from patron. No reply is deemed to be approval.

21	Bishop replies to patron giving approval of chosen candidate (go to step 24) or refuses approval (go to step 22).		Within 4 weeks of request from patron. No reply is deemed to be approval.
22	Patron, if refused approval for his chosen candidate, decides whether to ask the Archbishop of the province for the refusal to be reviewed (go to step 23). Alternatively the patron may consider other candidates (go to step 17).		
23	If requested to do so, the Archbishop investigates the matter and either overrides the refusal (go to step 24) or upholds the refusal (go to step 17).		
24	Patrol makes formal offer to priest chosen.		
25	Priest accepts offer.		
26	Patron gives notice of presentation to bishop. If within time limit go to step 33. If not go to step 27.	38	Within 9 months of the benefice becoming vacant.
27	If notice of presentation is not sent within 9 months of the vacancy then the right of presentation lapses to the Archbishop.		
28	Archbishop requests s11 statement, and any information he requires from bishop of diocese.		
29	Archbishop selects candidate. He might ask help or advice from diocesan bishop in this matter.		
30	Archbishop makes offer to priest.		
31	Priest accepts offer.		
32	Archbishop gives notice of presentation to diocesan bishop (go to step 33).		
33	Bishop may refuse to institute priest (go to step 34) or agree to do so (go to step 35).		
34	Patron or priest may appeal to Archbishop and Dean of the Arches. If they allow the appeal go to step 35. If they refuse the appeal go to step 17. (This is a residual right from earlier legislation and it is probable that if a bishop is not happy with the choice he is likely to use refusal under step 21 rather than wait till this late stage.)		
35	Bishop sends notification of proposed institution, with date if practicable, to Designated Officer, Registrar, priest, Archdeacon, and Rural Dean.		
36	Registrar notifies PCC secretary of date of institution.	17	
37	PCC secretary displays statutory notice of intention to institute or collate for 2 weeks. At the end of this period the secretary endorses the notice and returns it to the Registrar.	17	
38	Bishop institutes or collates the priest.		
39	A new ministry begins. Well done everyone!		

Appendix 4:
Some Useful Addresses

Clergy Appointments Adviser
Cowley House, Little College Street, Westminster SW1P 3SH
Tel: 0207 898 1898 Email: caa@c-of-e.org.uk

Patronage Secretary
Church Pastoral Aid Society
Athena Drive, Tachbrook Park, WARWICK CV34 6NG
Tel: 01926 458457

The Prime Minister's Appointment Secretary
& Ecclesiastical Secretary to the Lord Chancellor
(responsible for Crown patronage and Lord Chancellor's patronage)
10 Downing Street, LONDON SW1A 2AA
Tel: 0207 930 4433

Notes

1   The most notable exception concerns benefices where the Crown (defined as Her Majesty, the Duchy of Cornwall and the Duchy of Lancaster) or the Lord Chancellor is patron. They are exempt from this law's provisions. Nevertheless, those who are responsible for administering vacancies in these livings normally follow patterns of consultation and procedure very similar to the ones set out in the 1986 Measure.

2   It is equally possible for a bishop to dominate the process if he is sole patron. When that happens, our comments in the next paragraph (with the necessary adjustments) still apply.

3   The patron may, of course, be a member of the PCC. Even if not, he or she may feel a visit to the PCC is unnecessary if a section 12 meeting or something similar has been called.